A Tree Is a PLANT

by Clyde Robert Bulla

illustrated by Stacey Schuett

HarperCollins*Publishers*

For Gramps, with love

—S.S.

HarperCollins®, ☕®, and Let's-Read-and-Find-Out Science® are trademarks of HarperCollins Publishers Inc.

The *Let's-Read-and-Find-Out Science* book series was originated by Dr. Franklyn M. Branley, Astronomer Emeritus and former Chairman of the American Museum–Hayden Planetarium, and was formerly co-edited by him and Dr. Roma Gans, Professor Emeritus of Childhood Education, Teachers College, Columbia University. Text and illustrations for each of the books in the series are checked for accuracy by an expert in the relevant field. For more information on Let's-Read-and-Find-Out Science books, write to HarperCollins Children's Books, 1350 Avenue of the Americas, New York, NY 10019, or visit our website at www.letsreadandfindout.com.

A Tree Is a Plant

Library of Congress Cataloging-in-Publication Data
Bulla, Clyde Robert.
  A tree is a plant / by Clyde Robert Bulla ; illustrated by Stacey Schuett.
      p.   cm. — (Let's-read-and-find-out-science. Stage 1)
  Originally published: New York : Crowell, [1960].
ISBN 0-06-028171-5 — ISBN 0-06-028172-3 (lib. bdg.) — ISBN 0-06-445196-8 (pbk.)
  1. Apples—Life cycles—Juvenile literature.   2. Apples—Juvenile literature.   [1. Apples.   2. Trees.]
I. Schuett, Stacey, ill.   II. Title.   III. Series.
SB363.B785   2001
583'.73—dc21
                                                                                    00-040797
                                                                                    CIP
                                                                                    AC

Typography by Elynn Cohen   1 2 3 4 5 6 7 8 9 10   ❖   Newly Illustrated Edition

A Tree Is a Plant

CONIFER

MAPLE

PERSIMMON

PALMS

WILLOW

LEMON

A tree is a plant.

A tree is the biggest plant that grows.

Most kinds of trees grow from seeds the way most small plants do.

There are many kinds of trees.

Here are a few of them.

How many do you know?

This tree grows in the country. It might grow in your yard, too.

Do you know what kind it is?

This is an apple tree.

This apple tree came from a seed.

The seed was small.

It grew inside an apple.

Have you ever seen an apple seed?

Ask an adult to help you cut an apple in two.

The seeds are in the center.

They look like this.

Most apple trees come from seeds that are planted.

Sometimes an apple tree grows from a seed that falls to the ground.

The wind blows leaves over the seed.
The wind blows soil over the seed.

All winter the seed lies under the leaves and the soil.
All winter the seed lies under the ice and snow and
is pushed into the ground.

Spring comes.
Rain falls.
The sun comes out and warms the earth.
The seed begins to grow.

9

At first the young plant does not look like a tree.

The tree is very small.

It is only a stem with two leaves.

It has no apples on it.

A tree must grow up before it has apples on it.

Each year the tree grows. It grows tall.

In seven years it is so tall that you can
stand under its branches.

In the spring there are blossoms on the tree.

Spring is apple-blossom time.

11

The blossoms last only a few days.
Then they fall to the ground.
Now there are green leaves on the tree. Among the leaves there
are small apples. The apples are where the blossoms were before.
The apples are green, and they are almost too small for you to see.
The apples grow slowly.

They grow all during the spring and the summer.
In the fall they are large and ripe. They are ready to eat.

We can see the apples and the leaves on the branches.

We can see the branches growing out of the trunk.

We can see the trunk growing out of the ground.

We can see the bark of the tree.

The bark covers the branches and the trunk like a coat.

But there is a part of the tree that we cannot see.

We cannot see the roots.

They are under the ground.

Some of the roots are large.

Some of them are as small as hairs.

The roots grow like branches under the ground.

A tree could not live without roots.

Roots hold the trunk in the ground.

Roots keep the tree from falling when the wind blows.

Roots keep the rain from washing the tree out of the ground.

Roots do something more. They take water from the ground.

They carry the water into the trunk of the tree.

The trunk carries the water to the branches.

The branches carry the water to the leaves.

20

Hundreds and hundreds of leaves grow on the branches. The leaves make food from water and air. They make food when the sun shines.

The food goes into the branches. It goes into the trunk and roots. It goes to every part of the tree.

Fall comes and winter is near.
The work of the leaves is over.

The leaves turn yellow
and brown.
The leaves die and fall
to the ground.

22

Now the tree is bare.
All winter it looks dead.
But the tree is not dead.
Under its coat of bark,
the tree is alive.

Spring comes again. Rain falls.

The sun warms the earth.
The tree blossoms, and new leaves grow.
As long as it lives, the apple tree grows.
As long as it lives, the apple tree blossoms
in the spring, and apples grow on it.

When do you like apple trees best?

In spring when they are covered with blossoms?

In summer when they are covered with leaves?

In winter when they are bare?

Or in fall when they are covered with apples?

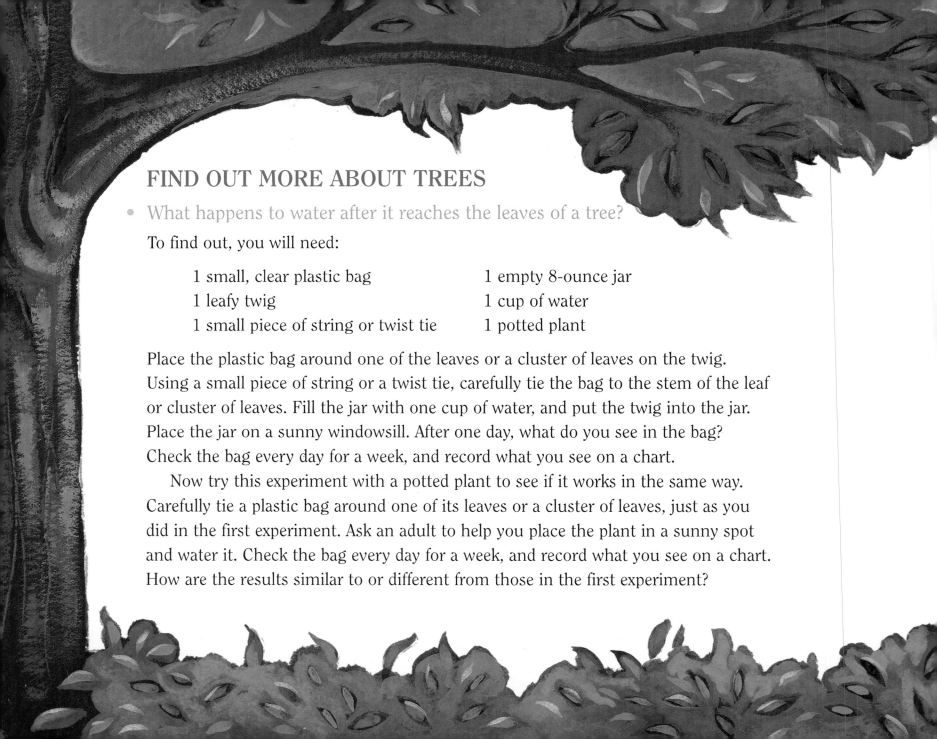

FIND OUT MORE ABOUT TREES

- What happens to water after it reaches the leaves of a tree?

To find out, you will need:

1 small, clear plastic bag	1 empty 8-ounce jar
1 leafy twig	1 cup of water
1 small piece of string or twist tie	1 potted plant

Place the plastic bag around one of the leaves or a cluster of leaves on the twig. Using a small piece of string or a twist tie, carefully tie the bag to the stem of the leaf or cluster of leaves. Fill the jar with one cup of water, and put the twig into the jar. Place the jar on a sunny windowsill. After one day, what do you see in the bag? Check the bag every day for a week, and record what you see on a chart.

Now try this experiment with a potted plant to see if it works in the same way. Carefully tie a plastic bag around one of its leaves or a cluster of leaves, just as you did in the first experiment. Ask an adult to help you place the plant in a sunny spot and water it. Check the bag every day for a week, and record what you see on a chart. How are the results similar to or different from those in the first experiment?

- How old is your tree?

Trees can live for a very long time. The trees in your backyard or in the park may be as old as you are or they may be as old as your grandpa or grandma—or even older! Some trees can live longer than others. Redwood trees, which grow in northern California, can live an average of 600 years. The oldest known redwood was 2,200 years old!

To find the age of a tree, wrap a tape measure around the trunk about three feet above the ground. The distance that you are measuring around the middle of a tree is called the girth. Every inch in the girth equals about one year in a tree's growth. How old is your tree? Is it younger or older than you are? By how many years?

- Read more about trees and plants

You can learn more about trees and plants in these great books:
A TREE IS GROWING by Arthur Dorros, illustrated by S. D. Schindler
HOW A SEED GROWS by Helene J. Jordan, illustrated by Loretta Krupinski
HOW DO APPLES GROW? by Betsy Maestro, illustrated by Giulio Maestro